You're IT!

With ♥ & hope ~

The Little Boy Who Found IT

A Story of Heart and Hope

the little IT series

Janae Bower

illustrated by Lynette Daniel

Andover, MN

ISBN 13: 978-1-931945-50-9
ISBN 10: 1-931945-50-0

Library of Congress Catalog Number: 2005937935

Printed in Korea

First Printing: February 2006

10 09 08 07 06   6 5 4 3 2 1

Expert Publishing, Inc.
14314 Thrush Street NW, Andover, MN 55304-3330
1-877-755-4966
www.expertpublishinginc.com

To order, visit *www.findingIT.com*
Quantity discounts available.

Keepsake Page

To: _____

From: _____

Receiving it warms the heart.

Reading it inspires hope.

Dedication

Dedicated to my son, **Gavin**, whose birth
inspired me to write this book.

In memory of my father-in-law, **John Sr.**,
who illustrated the first book
of the series, *The Little Girl
Who Found IT: A Story of Heart
and Hope*, and unexpectedly
died before he could illustrate
this book.

This was the last picture John Sr. drew in honor of his grandson, Gavin.

There once was a little boy just as happy as can be

His life was filled with joy and love when he was young and free.

Being so young
Playing a ton

4

Loving everyone.

Never in a hurry
Never with a worry

Living IT was fun.

But suddenly
something changed.

8

The little boy grew up.

9

What he did as a little boy
No longer brought him the same joy.

Oh how he longed
To be big and strong.

Playing with other big boys
Meant having lots of big toys.

IT was important to be cool
Only being with friends that rule.

Always in a hurry—
who had time to wait
with games to play,
cars to drive,
and girls to date?

14

There were many things to worry about,
Being the best at all he did—no doubt.

Everything he did, he did so he'd fit in,
Otherwise he would never find IT again.

He was as happy
as could be
Living how he thought
IT should be.

But suddenly
something
changed.

The little boy
grew up more.

Everything started
to change
His teen years seemed
so strange.

He decided to go far away
On his own—no rules to obey.

He studied hard
and had lots of fun;
Why didn't he get IT with school done?

Up the corporate ladder he soon started to climb
Striving to go far and reach the top in no time.

Beating the competition is what he believed
Is the way to get IT with all he achieved.

When IT didn't come
with the money,

It was time to look
for a honey.

He had fun when he wanted to date
Finally finding his life-long mate.

26

Then they married with his wife at his side
Ready for the future he would provide.

Their first new home soon came more alive
With each of their kids—a total of five.

He was as happy as could be
Living how he thought IT should be.

But suddenly
something changed.

30

The little boy grew old.

31

IT was time to retire—that he knew
Yet not sure what IT is or what to do.

He took it easy and had no stress;
Still not finding IT made him a mess.

The only way to get rid of this strife
Was to focus on the important things in life.

When his grandson came over to play,
He finally knew why he missed
IT along the way.

And suddenly he changed!

The little boy
grew wise.

This is what he needed to say with what he's learned along the way,

"All my life I've been looking for IT, now it's plain to see
To live a life of heart and hope, IT has to start with me!"

IT can't come from others, IT comes from within, A special part of you that has always been.

When you believe in yourself and in the One above,
Your life will be full of meaning, joy, peace, and love.

Your heart will shine; hope will grow.
IT's a journey—long and slow.

My journey started young and free;
IT was inside, a part of me.

I grew up and as a teen
I had to compete
In order to find IT
and be complete.

The more I grew up,
the more I believed

IT was something to be
bought and achieved.

When I grew old with nothing to control,
I let go and let IT inside make me whole.

When IT comes from the heart of you,
Then there is hope in all you do.

He was as happy as happy as can be
Finally living life the way IT ought to be!

The End

Special Acknowledgements

My heartfelt thanks and appreciation to:

Lynette Daniel, the talented illustrator, for continuing my father-in-law's legacy by modeling the illustrations from the first book.

The boys of all ages in my life—especially my husband, son, father, and brother—whose life journeys are an inspiration.

Family and friends, for the gift of precious support and feedback with the book.

Richard Leider, whose amazing work around IT helped me find IT!

Harry and Sharron Stockhausen, the publishers, and Sara Weingartner, the graphic designer, for the gift of bringing this book to life.

Author

Janae Bower is an inspirational teacher and business consultant. She is the author of the award-winning book, *The Little Girl Who Found IT: A Story of Heart and Hope*, the first book in the series. Janae lives in Minnesota with her husband, John, and son, Gavin.

Order Information

Give the gift of these books
to your family
and friends.

Email janae@findingIT.com or go to
www.findingIT.com for:

- ordering information
- keepsake products
- fundraising options
- presentations and workshops